COLONIAL CONCORD

A STUDY IN PEN AND INK

JAMES H. DEE JR.

CONCORD, MASSACHUSETTS

Fourth Printing, 1964

THE MURRAY PRINTING COMPANY, FORGE VILLAGE, MASSACHUSETTS

FOREWORD

It seems a characteristic trait of human beings everywhere to manifest at some time or other an almost invincible urge and desire to return to those wonderful places of their youth and past where memories closest to their hearts are fondly recalled. Thus, each year the world bears witness to a tremendous exodus of travellers everywhere returning to their beloved homes; home to the little churches nestled in the countryside where first they knew the indescribable bliss of love and marriage; home to the schools and familiar byways of their youth, filled with a thousand memories that never fail; many return to that cabin in the hills, or the rambling country home, or the farm, the tenement, any one of a thousand places where first they knew the sweet rapture of living, where youth returns once more in all its haunting beauty. There they may recapture again the joy, the pride, the happiness of a youth once lived, but ever lost in the unrelenting march of time.

And thus do many come home to old Concord town year after year, not home to the place they were born perhaps, but home to the place where their own native land first breathed the air of independence and freedom. Here in the "birthplace of American independence" they experience another emotion, this of a deeper and more significant tone, a pride and joy associated with patriotism and love of country that raises a man's spirit and fills his heart with a bursting pride and deepening loyalty. For here in this small unpretentious New England town on the morning of April 19, 1775 a small band of courageous Patriots stood their ground against a superior contingent of British Redcoats, driving them back from that "rude bridge that arched the flood," driving them back towards Lexington and Boston and eventually back to Britain itself. And so it is with this profound emotion of heartfelt pride and joy that so many visit old Concord town each year, many for the first time, to breathe anew the sweet air of freedom and independence, to tread across that same bridge that once echoed the steady march of the "embattled farmers," to look up into the face of the Minuteman and read there the history of a new nation, to read there the determination, purpose and destiny of a man at a plow, musket in hand, ready to die for an ideal, a principle, a new nation, a way of life.

Though more famous for the great historical event that here transpired, Concord is renowned also as a literary center. Such notable writers as Emerson, Thoreau, Hawthorne, the Alcotts, Channing and others have left the town a heritage of literary genius that has charmed and enraptured America for many years. Here in this little Colonial town the eminent philosopher Emerson mused upon the nature of man, the soul, being and reality, leaving behind writings of the deepest feeling and insight; here at peaceful Walden roamed at random the famous naturalist, Henry David Thoreau, a great lover of nature who saw in the creation about him a meaning and message few have ever grasped; here wrote the Alcotts their charming stories of family life and love; here close by at the Wayside wrote Nathaniel Hawthorne and Margaret Sydney, pouring forth from prolific pens those delightful and charming intrigues of fictionalized reality. How proud is Concord of her history and tradition; how proud is Concord of her writers and literature; how proud should all Americans be of this little town, for here was born freedom, here was "fired the shot heard round the world," here is celebrated the birth of a nation, our nation, America the beautiful!

Now from the talented pen of a young Concord artist, James H. Dee Jr., have emanated these remarkable etchings of the famous points of interest found throughout the town. Mr. Dee has truly captured the spirit of Colonial antiquity and charm in these beautiful drawings and attached to them a singular flair of artistic interpretation and emotion. A native of Concord all his life, Mr. Dee has spent long, tedious hours over his drawings and in the true tradition of art has poured his very being into his skilled interpretations, giving old Concord town one of the finest collections of pen and ink sketches ever to have appeared here.

DANA C. PIERCE.

TO MY WIFE AND CHILDREN

THIS BOOK

IS FONDLY DEDICATED

The Minuteman

This beautiful bronze statue, artistically fashioned by the same man, Daniel Chester French, who sculptured the handsome replica of Abraham Lincoln in his Memorial at Washington, D.C., was solemnly dedicated on the centennial anniversary of the Concord battle. At this spot Major John Buttrick gave the order to fire upon the British militia and the "shot heard round the world" echoed its victorious blast across the adjacent valley as the first great war for the American ideals of freedom and liberty began.

This particular statue became a familiar sight to Americans throughout the country, when during the course of World War II it was chosen as one of the patriotic symbols for the War Bond drives.

Viewed by thousands of tourists year after year, the Minuteman stands in resolute pride and courage gazing boldly across the bridge he once defended that America might live and prosper as a free nation.

BY THE RUDE BRIDGE THAT
ARCHED THE FLOOD
THEIR FLAG TO APRIL'S
BREEZE UNFURLED
HERE ONCE THE EMBATTLED
FARMERS STOOD
AND FIRED THE SHOT HEARD
ROUND THE WORLD

The Bullet Hole House

In Colonial days this home was owned by Elisha Jones, who stored supplies and ammunition within for the Minutemen in case of just such emergency as was the Revolution. During the battle a stray bullet struck the house and lodged there and the place where it is imbedded can be seen till this day. Close upon this site there still remains the stone across which Capt. Isaac Davis fell, victim of an enemy bullet. The home is one of the oldest in Concord, the original part of the main house having been built by John Smedley, a first settler.

The wife of one of Colonel Barret's grandsons lived here many years ago. She used to relate her vivid recollections of that day on which the British Redcoats marched by her very door, while she sat upon a pile of salt fish, which formed a part of the stores concealed within this old Concord home.

Still privately owned, the Bullet Hole House remains one of the town's most historic spots, seemingly as indestructible as the history which has made it one of the most historic homes in America.

The Battle Monument

This granite monument marks the approximate spot where the British soldiers fired their first volleys at the American Patriots across the river. Dedicated to the memory of the heroic Minutemen who fought and died here, the words inscribed thereon, composed in part by Mr. Emerson, read as follows:

HERE

ON THE 19TH OF APRIL,

1775

WAS MADE

THE FIRST FORCEABLE RESISTANCE

TO BRITISH AGGRESSION.

ON THE OPPOSITE BANK

STOOD THE AMERICAN MILITIA.

HERE STOOD THE INVADING ARMY;

AND ON THIS SPOT

THE FIRST OF THE ENEMY FELL

IN THE WAR OF THAT REVOLUTION

WHICH GAVE

INDEPENDENCE

TO THESE UNITED STATES.

IN GRATITUDE TO GOD

AND

IN THE LOVE OF FREEDOM

THIS MONUMENT

WAS ERECTED

A.D. 1836.

The Old Manse

Built even prior to the Revolution, the Old Manse was destined to provide lodging for several of the famous Concord writers. Ralph Waldo Emerson's grandfather, the Rev. William Emerson, a famous Concord minister, built this home and actually looked out upon the historic battle that took place here close by from one of his windows overlooking the battleground. Ralph Waldo Emerson also lived here in the Old Manse and composed many of his early poems, as well as his first published book, "Nature." Later Nathaniel Hawthorne occupied the home and wrote his celebrated work, "Mosses from an Old Manse."

In the room just above the dining room Emerson wrote his "Nature" and many of his best poems. Hawthorne also used this room as his personal study, a description of which appears in his "Mosses from an Old Manse," which was also written here.

The Manse is now a famous Concord landmark for literary enthusiasts who throng here in ever-increasing numbers to pay respect to the great writers of the past who once lived, thought and wrote within this very home.

The Old North Bridge

Here at this bridge on the fateful morning of April 19, 1775 rang aloud the crack of American and British muskets in the first gallant action of the Revolutionary War. Just across this bridge stood a handful of bold and courageous American Minutemen, ready to die for a country as yet unborn. Some fell here, immortal heroes, but not in vain, as the red-coated British militia was dispersed in a rout fleeing towards Lexington, beaten severely by the invincible spirit of these gallant Colonial Patriots; beaten by a spirit that shortly afterwards gave birth to a new nation.

Now no longer does this historic bridge resound to the determined tread of marching feet. Instead a steady stream of patriotic Americans files across the bridge each year, pausing for a moment in solemn and silent tribute to the brave men that here fell that America might live as a free nation.

The Colonial Inn

This old Colonial building was once the center of great activity in the days just prior to the Revolution, for here were kept many of the arms, provisions and other war materials used in defense of British aggression on that historic morning of April 19, 1775.

The building is now known as the Colonial Inn and is one of the most popular places in town to spend a pleasant night's lodging or partake of a hearty repast.

The Management has succeeded in preserving the Colonial atmosphere to a high degree within, where many relics of the Revolutionary period may still be seen.

An interesting note concerning the Inn is that the Thoreau family at one time occupied a portion of the original edifice.

Situated at the head of Monument Square, the Inn looks out upon the stately Concord monument dedicated to the memory of those heroes who died in the Civil War. Now one of the town's notable landmarks itself, the Colonial Inn delights in entertaining the host of tourists and travellers who wend their way to Concord each year to see the many historic and literary points of interest.

The Wright Tavern

Built in 1747 the Wright Tavern still stands in dignified repose on its original site overlooking the Mill Dam. In this tavern the Patriots made their headquarters on the morning of April 19, 1775, though later in the day it was occupied by the British militia. Legend has it that here the Britisher Major Pitcairn, as he stirred his morning dram, swore that "before the day was over he would stir the damned Yankee blood as well."

The Tavern still maintains its air of Colonial independence and charm despite the passing years. One of the town's most famous and historic buildings, the Tavern is now doubly interesting, having become an antique center as well as a conventional inn.

Just across the street from the Tavern is situated the Old Hill Burying Ground, final resting place of many of the early Concord settlers, while just to the other side stands the First Parish Meeting House, where the First Provincial Congress took place in October, 1774.

The Old Hill Burying Ground

In this old burying ground were buried many of the early settlers of Concord. The headstones are noted for their curious and moralizing epitaphs, probably most famous of which is that of John Jack, an old negro slave who died in Concord in 1773. His famous epitaph reads in part:

"GOD WILLS US FREE, MAN WILLS US SLAVES,
I WILL AS GOD WILLS, GOD'S WILL BE DONE."

The oldest stone in the burying ground is probably that of Joseph Merriam, who died the twentieth of April, 1677.

On the stone wall just below the burying ground the following words are inscribed:

ON THIS HILL
THE SETTLERS OF CONCORD
BUILT THEIR MEETING HOUSE
NEAR WHICH THEY WERE BURIED.
ON THE SOUTHERN SLOPE OF THE RIDGE
WERE THEIR DWELLINGS DURING THE FIRST WINTER.
BEFORE IT THEY LAID OUT THEIR FIRST ROAD AND ON
THE SUMMIT STOOD THE
LIBERTY POLE OF THE REVOLUTION.

Indicative of the curious epitaphs found therein, this one being on the first white stone which was placed in the cemetery, is that inscribed on the headstone of Miss Abigail Dudley. It reads as follows:

THIS STONE IS DESIGNED
BY ITS DURABILITY
TO PERPETUATE THE MEMORY,
AND BY ITS COLOUR
TO SIGNIFY THE MORAL CHARACTER
OF
MISS ABIGAIL DUDLEY.

The Melvin Memorial

This beautiful memorial, Mourning Victory, is another of the many remarkable works of art sculptured by Daniel Chester French. It is dedicated to the memory of the three Melvin brothers, who ventured from Concord to join the forces engaged in the Civil War. Theirs was a journey destined to lead to immortality and none returned. Thus a fourth brother deemed it fitting to perpetuate their memory through the medium of this outstanding piece of sculpture.

The Memorial is situated in the Sleepy Hollow Cemetery, not far from the center of town, where several of the Concord authors were also laid to rest. Among these are Emerson, Thoreau, Hawthorne and Alcott.

French, the sculptor and a native of Exeter, New Hampshire, became one of the nation's most celebrated artists during the course of his lifetime. His handsome "Minuteman," also situated in Concord, as well as the colossal bronze "Lincoln" for the Lincoln Memorial at Washington, are merely two of his many outstanding works that have brought him lasting fame and admiration.

The Art Center

This old Colonial home, built before 1753 by John Ball, houses the many fine exhibitions of the Concord Art Association. This Society has succeeded in acquiring many fine works of art, which are periodically on display along with exhibits and works borrowed from other galleries and private owners.

Situated on Lexington Road, close to the center of town, the building itself lends an atmosphere of antiquity and charm to the town, being one of the finer examples of the large Colonial home so typical of Concord in the earlier days of its existence.

At one period of its existence this building was a link in the "underground railroad," which spirited so many oppressed slaves northward to the Canadian sanctuary. Secret passageways and rooms within harbored these slaves from those authorities attempting to thwart their reckless escapades to freedom.

It is truly fitting and appropriate that a home of such outstanding grace and beauty should house the many beautiful works of art collected by the Concord Art Association.

The First Parish Church

This historic Colonial church was built on the very same wooden frame of the building that housed the First Provincial Congress on the fourteenth of October, 1775. None other than the estimable John Hancock was chosen president of this particular Congress. Here in this building rang forth the persuasive orations of Hancock, Adams and other Colonial Patriots, fired by the spirit of freedom and independence.

As early as 1636 this church was organized at Cambridge, and in 1637, the Rev. Peter Bulkeley and John Jones were chosen as teacher and pastor. Later the eloquent Patriot, Rev. William Emerson, preached here for many years.

This church is one of the finest examples of the Colonial type church found throughout New England. It has become a favorite subject for photographer and artist alike and has appeared several times in national publications.

Steeped in the tradition and history of old Concord town, this old meetinghouse remains one of the more famous landmarks of the town, still somehow maintaining an aura of freedom and sanctity.

The Home of Emerson

In this modest country home the eminent poet and philosopher, Ralph Waldo Emerson, lived from the year 1835 till that of his death in 1882. One of America's most famous philosophers and thinkers, Emerson engendered a sizeable following not only in this country, but also abroad where he was likewise held in the greatest esteem. Though dead now many years, the spirit of Emerson somehow seems to survive and his influence even to this day is noted and felt in intellectual circles.

A great lover of nature and his fellow man, Emerson endeared himself to all with whom he came in contact. His home was perpetually filled with a host of friends and associates, including many of the great literary figures of his time. Henry David Thoreau was a frequent visitor at his home and the two spent many profound hours in long walks through the surrounding countryside or within the study where Emerson wrote and thought with such diligence and insight.

Concord's most famous and dearly beloved citizen, Emerson lives on in the minds and hearts of many the world over, all of whom have recognized the genius and wisdom of the man who stamped his own immortality here in this little New England town so many years ago.

The Orchard House

Home of the famous Alcott family, the Orchard House presents an historic study in tradition and literature. Here Amos Bronson Alcott raised his famous family, most renowned of which was Louisa May, celebrated author of "Little Women" and numerous other works. Alcott himself moved in literary and intellectual circles, making a considerable name for himself in the field of education.

This home is also the birthplace of the "Concord School of Philosophy," begun here in 1879. Later on the quaint chapel just to the rear of the house was built to hold the expanding sessions of the little school, where Emerson and other learned scholars of the day delivered their profound philosophical dissertations.

Immediately adjacent to the Orchard House stands Hawthorne's Wayside, another famous literary shrine. The proximity of two such literary stalwarts as Louisa May Alcott and Nathaniel Hawthorne in the same town was indeed a most remarkable coincidence.

Hawthorne's Wayside

In 1852 Nathaniel Hawthorne moved to Concord from Salem, Massachusetts and purchased this home situated about a mile from the center of town. In the hopes of finding a quiet and secluded spot where he might write and contemplate, Hawthorne had the tower room built much in the manner of one he had seen earlier while travelling in Italy. There in the seclusion and quiet he so loved he wrote many of his outstanding works that have so endeared him to his host of admirers.

Some years after Hawthorne's death the renowned publisher Daniel Lothrop secured this home from his daughter. It was his wife, writing under the pseudonym of Margaret Sydney, who wrote the much heralded and dearly beloved children's books among which were "Five Little Peppers" and "The Little Maid of Concord Town."

The Wayside is truly rich in literature and tradition, and it is with just cause that it has become one of the most sacred literary shrines in the country.

Thoreau's Cairn

These stone pillars mark the site of the humble abode of the hermit poet and philosopher, Henry David Thoreau, who roamed in deepest thought and meditation the area about this spot and his beloved Walden Pond. Here Thoreau spent many an hour contemplating the meaning and beauty of the nature that surrounded him, jotting in his diary many of his profound observations of the great drama of life, nature and creation that transpired about him. He lived here under many discomforting hardships, yet they were hardships that he bore, even reveled in, since they brought him that intimate union with nature he so craved.

Thoreau's way of life had its message, however. A sincere and profound philosopher, he wished to protest by the simplicity of his habits and way of life the folly of man in devoting so much time to society and superficial living. Thus did he take to the woods of Walden where he lived a life devoted to simplicity and an appreciation of nature and creation, hoping against hope that man might find by his example the folly of his ways.

The beauty of Walden and the surrounding countryside and woodlands has lost little of its appeal since the day of Thoreau, still evincing an aura of enchantment and charm as it did in those days when this renowned Concord naturalist lived here in the solitude and peace of nature.

The Antiquarian Society

In this building are preserved many of old Concord's most famous and interesting mementoes. Built by the Concord Antiquarian Society, which was incorporated in 1887, the interior is arranged much in the manner of an old Colonial residence with many quaint pieces of furniture and articles of great historic interest. The collection of old china and furniture within is one of the most interesting of the exhibits on display. Another fine exhibit in the museum is the antiquarian collection of Cummings E. Davis, purchased by the Society in 1886.

Here within the walls of this historic old museum still lives the spirit of old Concord. It has become one of the favorite stopping places for the thousands of tourists who flock to Concord each year.

With each passing year the treasures of the museum become more valuable and precious, and so it is with great personal pride and vigor that the Trustees of the Society maintain this museum that the great history of old Concord town may somehow live on in these old Colonial exhibits which link the present with Revolutionary days.

The Grapevine Cottage

In this cozy little cottage lived Ephraim Wales Bull, the discoverer of the now famous Concord grape. The grape was produced by a scientific process known as hybridizing. It is generally reputed to be a cross between the Isabella and the native wild grape. Close by a tablet memorializing this historic discovery reads as follows:

EPHRAIM WALES BULL

PLANTED THE SEED OF A

WILD LABRUSCA GRAPE

FOUND GROWING ON

THIS HILLSIDE

WHICH

AFTER THREE GENERATIONS

THROUGH HIS WORK

AND WISDOM

BECAME

IN THIS GARDEN

IN SEPTEMBER, 1849

THE

CONCORD GRAPE

The Concord Monument

The Soldiers' Monument, erected on Monument Square on April 19, 1867, was dedicated to the memory of those courageous men who gave their lives in the Civil War. The appropriate tribute, "Faithful Unto Death," is carved in high relief on the south side of the monument. On the north side the dates 1861 to 1865 are inscribed, while on the eastern side are found the words:

THE

TOWN OF CONCORD

BUILDS THIS MONUMENT

IN HONOR OF

THE BRAVE MEN

WHOSE NAMES IT BEARS

AND RECORDS

WITH GRATEFUL PRIDE

THAT THEY FOUND HERE

A BIRTHPLACE, HOME OR GRAVE.

1866

On the west side of the monument a bronze tablet bears the names of those heroes who died that their country might persevere in unity and freedom for all.

The Concord Free Public Library

The Library is one of the town's most beautiful buildings, situated at an excellent vantage point close to the center of town. It was first organized in 1873 and funds were set aside for its maintenance by William Munroe, a wealthy citizen and native of the town.

Several other legacies have been donated to the Library, making provisions for books, the art collections and various other uses. Not only has the Library an excellent, well-rounded selection of books, but many of the literary masterpieces of the Concord authors and historic relics are preserved there in great pride.

The handsome life-size statue of Emerson, sculptured by Daniel Chester French, is a permanent fixture in the main lobby of the Library. Several sculptured busts of other eminent Concord writers and citizens form a solemn ring about the same lobby, lending an air of intense thought and deep knowledge to the Library as a whole.

Separate alcoves are set aside for the famous Concord authors and many interesting souvenirs and mementoes of Colonial days can also be seen within.

The Concord River

One would have to travel many a mile before he would find a river as calm, peaceful and serene as the old Concord River. As in the days of her historic past this lovely stream flows idly by, wending its way on to the Merrimac and thence to the sea. The peace that now pervades its course and banks subtly belies the fierce action that took place here so many years ago. But history does not lie and gives ample testimony to the historic event that happened close by on the morning of April 19, 1775. On that day her peaceful waters ran red as American and British blood united in the great paradox of war, as the Patriots and Redcoats bitterly engaged in the first violent action of the American Revolution. Now once again her waters run peacefully by in a free country, born here on her banks on that fateful morning long ago.

Overlooking the river is the beautiful Buttrick estate, home of one of Concord's oldest and finest families, celebrated in both its history and tradition since Revolutionary days.